BABY STEPS

BABY STEPS

ELARA PHOENIX

CONTENTS

CHAPTER 1

Introduction to Child Development

Child development is a combination of both anatomical and psychological changes that occur in children during their early years. These changes, influenced by the intricate dance between nature (genetics) and nurture (environment), shape how a child grows into their unique self. Understanding child development is crucial for parents, educators, and health professionals to ensure children achieve their full potential.

The Interplay of Nature and Environment

Children's development results from the constant interplay between their genetic makeup and environmental influences. Genetics provide the blueprint, but the environment molds and modifies this blueprint. This dual influence means each child's development path is unique, filled with its own pace, detours, and milestones.

Monitoring Developmental Progress

Given the individuality in growth, it's important to track how children develop across various domains:

- **Language Development:** Watching for a child's ability to understand and use language. This includes vocabulary size, sentence structure, and the ability to communicate needs and thoughts effectively.

- **Motor Development:** Observing both fine motor skills (such as picking up small objects and writing) and gross motor skills (like crawling, walking, and jumping).
- **Cognitive Development:** Assessing how children think, explore, and figure things out. It involves problem-solving, memory, and decision-making abilities.
- **Socio-Emotional Development:** Understanding how children manage emotions, develop self-awareness, and build relationships with others.

The Unique Pace of Development

Every child grows and matures at their own pace. Development is not linear; skills in different areas often overlap and evolve without a set pattern. Thus, understanding and respecting this unique pace is essential for those monitoring a child's growth.

The Role of Milestones

To guide this monitoring, child development milestones act as a helpful roadmap. These are average indicators of what most children can do at specific ages. They provide a checklist for parents and professionals to track whether a child is developing as expected. However, while they serve as a helpful tool, they should not be the sole measure of a child's development.

Key Developmental Areas

At different ages, certain key areas are examined to ensure healthy development:

- **Movement and Muscle Development:** Tracking physical abilities and coordination.

- **Emotional Development:** Understanding a child's emotional responses and coping mechanisms.
- **Learning and Cognitive Skills:** Monitoring a child's ability to learn new concepts and solve problems.
- **Communication and Language:** Observing how a child communicates with others and their ability to understand language.
- **Social Relationships:** Watching how a child interacts with peers and adults.

Addressing Developmental Delays

Monitoring these signs over time helps in identifying developmental delays early. If a child doesn't meet expected milestones, it might indicate a developmental issue. Early intervention is crucial; it can transform what could be a challenging and uncertain period into an opportunity for targeted support and growth.

Importance of Detailed Tracking

Detailed tracking of development is especially vital for children showing signs of delay. It provides the most reliable resource to ensure they receive the necessary support and intervention, thereby reducing stress for both the child and family.

CHAPTER 2

The Importance of Tracking Milestones

Parents and caregivers consider it extremely important to track their baby's developmental milestones or little successes. Up to around the age of three, this tracking is crucial; beyond that, constant comparison can be detrimental to everyone involved. Pediatricians place a high priority on measuring growth to ensure that children remain on target and achieve the same milestones as their peers. This is vital, as 16-20% of children need extra help due to developmental delays. Early identification and intervention are key to minimizing impact and helping re-align children with a standard development timeline.

Early Identification and Intervention

Early identification and intervention can significantly reduce the impact of developmental delays. Monitoring milestones helps keep things in perspective and provides context for observations. For instance, if a daycare teacher mentions that your child is behind peers in learning to walk, it's important not to panic. Children often experience dramatic developmental expansions over short periods, so rushing to judgment can lead to unnecessary anxiety.

The Role of Multiple Milestones

In tracking growth, it's essential to use multiple milestones to guide healthy child development. While children do not all develop at the same speed, there are significant alerts and landmarks that indicate their progression. For example, if a child hasn't started talking by age three, comparing them to peers might prompt parents to consult an audiologist to check for hearing issues. This proactive approach can identify underlying issues early, allowing for timely intervention.

Understanding Variations in Development

Different children may exhibit significant variations in their developmental timelines. Some children may appear to lag behind in certain areas, only to catch up dramatically within a short period. Recognizing these patterns and understanding the broader context is crucial.

Addressing Language Milestones

Language milestones are particularly important to track. If a child struggles with phonological processing while peers seem to master language effortlessly, early intervention can prevent compounded developmental delays. Understanding a child's unique developmental path allows for tailored support that addresses specific needs and fosters optimal growth.

The Impact of Context

Context is critical when assessing developmental milestones. For example, if a child shows signs of delayed language development, considering their environment, previous experiences, and overall health can provide crucial insights. This holistic approach helps in applying appropriate interventions early on, potentially preventing long-term issues and supporting the child's overall well-being.

Detailed Tracking and Its Benefits

Detailed tracking is especially vital for children showing signs of developmental delays. It ensures they receive the necessary support and intervention, reducing stress for both the child and family. This proactive approach aligns children with a healthy development trajectory, ensuring they reach their full potential.

CHAPTER 3

Physical Development Milestones

Children grow and change dramatically in their first few years of life. They can grow as much as 10 inches in just the first year! By age 5, many children will have doubled their birth height. Along with physical growth, their movements evolve significantly during this period. From rolling over as infants to jumping as toddlers, they achieve numerous physical milestones marking major progress in their motor development. This section explores the typical physical growth of children's bodies and their movement as they approach each milestone. We'll delve into gross motor skills, fine motor skills, and sensory development.

Understanding Individual Development

It's important to remember that typical development ranges widely, and not all children will reach milestones within the expected window. For instance, kids may begin to walk anywhere from 9 to 15 months of age. Some children might be more interested in kicking and catching a ball than in coloring or cutting. Additionally, some children may be sensitive to various sensations, while others may not notice them at all—and that's okay! Generally, however, the following sequences depict the range of skills we expect to see as children grow. No need to worry unless these sensory or motor milestones appear to be losing ground or stagnating altogether. Discuss any concerns or anomalies with your child's healthcare provider.

Gross Motor Skills

Gross motor skills involve the movement of large muscles in the body and are the cornerstone of physical development. The development of these skills begins at birth and typically continues until around age six, when fine motor skills and overall muscle control become more refined.

- **Newborn – 1 month:** A newborn typically has no voluntary control over their large muscles. However, infants' muscles quickly progress from some backward extension and flexion to varied, stable movements. They can lift their chest and head when placed on their tummy. The upper arms are barely off the chest, with elbows and knees bent.
- **2 – 3 months:** Extension increases, especially in the arms and head. The backs of the hands begin to close, though by 4 months, children still have some backward extension in their arms. The legs are exaggeratedly flexed, now moving forward enough to clear the table when lifting their legs.
- **4 – 5 months:** The end of backward extension in the arms signals the beginning of ball-throwing. Infants can extend their head enough to get a chin hold, then push off the floor to lift their chest and head for visual tracking. Refined control in the neck and upper body starts developing.
- **6 – 7 months:** Full control of large arm and hand muscles. With strong, stable muscles in the lower body to work against and more overall endurance to support these efforts, children begin challenging gravity in a range of gross motor activities.

Here are the milestones for gross motor development. Note that a child is not expected to have all these milestones at a specific age but should have most of them:

- Rolling over
- Sitting up without support
- Crawling
- Standing with assistance
- Walking with assistance
- Standing alone
- Walking alone
- Running
- Jumping
- Climbing stairs

Fine Motor Skills

Parents often take pride in their child's physical achievements: "He's crawling already!" "My little one can stand up." Watching children learn new physical skills brings a thrill of accomplishment. Fine motor skills involve the small muscle movements related to small body motions, hand-eye coordination, and dexterity. Mastery in these areas demonstrates precision and control, essential for self-care and play activities.

Fine Motor Milestones

- **1 month:** Babies' hands are mostly closed. Prevent them from reaching into their Tummy Time area to put objects into their mouth. Surveillance during Tummy Time helps the baby gain head strength, tone, and coordination to progress to hand games.

- **3 months:** Babies start to engage in the "hand by the face" game, boosting head strength and coordination.
- **6 months:** Babies begin to exhibit controlled hand movements, enhancing their fine motor control and coordination.

Sensory Development

Sensory development involves processing and integrating sensory information received through the body. There are several milestones in this area, including sensory processing and praxis. Sensory input is processed and acted upon via praxis, guiding movement. Typical development follows this progression:

- **Early months:** Babies can imitate faces made by adults, showing early mimicry and reciprocal interaction.
- **3-12 months:** Babies demonstrate a progression of skills related to sensory systems, engaging in social interactions and forming emotional attachments to caregivers. By 7 months, children can recognize their names and simple commands. Around this time, many babies start clapping to their favorite songs, coordinating movements with sounds.
- **9 months:** Babies develop the ability to suppress negative responses to fearful experiences and begin eating solid foods.
- **12 months:** Babies can verbalize simple wants, use gestures to communicate needs, and may wave in response to greetings.

CHAPTER 4

Cognitive Development Milestones

Cognitive development is one of the key areas that differentiate the early years of childhood. It encompasses several major components: language development, problem-solving, and memory. These elements play a crucial role in shaping how children perceive, understand, and interact with the world around them.

The Three Pillars of Cognitive Development

Language Development: This involves both speaking and understanding what others are saying. Children's language development progresses from basic sounds to complex sentences and includes both expressive language (speaking) and receptive language (understanding spoken words).

Problem Solving: Closely tied to memory, problem-solving is the ability to use knowledge, facts, and data to effectively solve problems. This skill develops significantly during early childhood, relying heavily on both short-term and long-term memory.

Memory: Divided into short-term and long-term phases, memory is essential for cognitive growth. Short-term memory is the main focus during early development, with infants and toddlers better at remembering events (procedural memory) rather than lists of words or factual information (semantic and episodic memory).

Language Development

Between birth and three months, babies start to learn how to use their vocal cords, producing various sounds and tones. This early vocal experimentation provides insight into the health of their vocal system, though it isn't a conscious attempt to mimic speech. Babies' gurgles and coos are rhythmic, concise, and easier to produce than human speech.

Throughout their second year, nonverbal communication skills remain strong. Babies will point, gesture, and use facial expressions, understanding up to ten times as many words as they use in speech. By age three, children's expressive vocabulary ranges from 200 to 1,000 words, and they speak in sentences three or four words long.

Language Development Milestones

- **Birth – 3 months:** Vocalizes with sounds like cooing and gurgling.
- **4 – 6 months:** Begins babbling and imitating sounds.
- **7 – 12 months:** Understands simple words and gestures; says simple words like "mama" and "dada."
- **1 – 2 years:** Vocabulary grows to 50-100 words; begins forming two-word sentences.
- **2 – 3 years:** Uses 200-1,000 words; forms three to four-word sentences; understands simple instructions.

Problem Solving and Memory

Problem Solving: Problem-solving development involves critical thinking and sequenced planning. Key factors include impulse control—resisting immediate temptations to achieve long-term goals. At 12 months, children engage in imitation solutions, mimicking correct solutions provided by adults and correcting their own actions.

Problem Solving Milestones

- **Birth – 3 months:** Begins to show interest in surroundings.
- **4 – 6 months:** Reaches for objects and explores them.
- **7 – 12 months:** Imitates simple actions; solves simple problems like finding a hidden toy.
- **1 – 2 years:** Engages in basic pretend play; solves more complex problems.
- **2 – 3 years:** Completes simple puzzles; begins to understand cause and effect.

Memory: Infants develop short-term memory (working memory), which includes the ability to remember auditory and visual input for a few seconds. Long-term memory also develops but is harder to assess. Initially, infants and toddlers excel at procedural memory (events) over semantic and episodic memory (facts and lists).

Memory Development Milestones

- **Birth – 3 months:** Recognizes familiar faces and objects.
- **4 – 6 months:** Remembers objects and people; recognizes sounds.
- **7 – 12 months:** Remembers locations of hidden objects; recognizes familiar routines.
- **1 – 2 years:** Repeats actions seen earlier; begins to form long-term memories.
- **2 – 3 years:** Remembers past events; can recall details from several months ago.

Creating a Supportive Environment

Understanding cognitive development helps parents create environments that foster growth. Providing diverse stimuli, encouraging exploration, and offering opportunities for problem-solving can significantly influence a child's cognitive development.

Monitoring Cognitive Milestones

Regular screenings and discussions with pediatricians ensure children are on track with their cognitive development. Simple assessments can detect deviations from typical developmental paths, allowing for early intervention and support.

CHAPTER 5

Social and Emotional Development Milestones

Children's emotional expressions often mirror their movements, a concept rooted in the Latin term "movēre." As toddlers become more mobile and expressive, their genuine thoughts and judgments become more apparent. Their social reasoning skills evolve through interactions and guided problem-solving.

Early Emotional and Social Development

From birth, babies begin to form social attributes such as adoration and affection. Eye contact, gazes, and responses from a parent build a relationship of trust and emotional connection, forming an incredible bond. This attachment is strengthened through shared moments of joy and comfort.

Early Milestones

The first major milestone in emotional and social development is forming an attachment bond. This begins at birth with the primary caregivers and evolves as the child grows.

- **Birth - 6 months:** Babies express emotions through cries, coos, and smiles. They begin to recognize familiar faces and respond to voices.

- **6 - 12 months:** Babies show preference for certain people, develop stranger anxiety, and begin to mimic expressions.
- **12 - 24 months:** Toddlers show a wide range of emotions, seek comfort from caregivers, and begin to show empathy by offering toys or patting a crying friend.

Attachment and Bonding

As children grow, they develop in five major areas: attachment and bonding, physical development, emotional development, questioning and inquiry, language development, and intellectual and cognitive development. Although each child develops at their own pace, these guidelines help indicate typical growth patterns.

Attachment is the bond between a parent and child that starts in utero. This early bond teaches an infant to trust that their needs will be met, which in turn, calms and satisfies the infant. A strong attachment leads to self-confidence and resilience later in life.

Attachment Milestones

- **Birth - 3 months:** Forms basic attachment through consistent care and comfort.
- **4 - 6 months:** Shows preference for primary caregiver.
- **7 - 12 months:** Develops stranger anxiety and stronger attachment to primary caregiver.
- **1 - 2 years:** Seeks comfort from caregivers, shows affection.

Empathy and Social Skills

Empathy and social skills develop as children interact with others and understand their own and others' emotions. Preschoolers, for example, begin to show empathy, like the child who suggested including a friend in a game, demonstrating a growing understanding of others' feelings.

Developing Empathy

1. **Model Empathy:** Share your feelings and talk about others' emotions. "I'm excited for the weekend plans with friends I haven't seen in a while. I've missed having that in-person quality time."
2. **Share Memories:** Sharing genuine childhood memories can build empathy. "A grade school buddy reached out, and I realized how much he helped me back then. Thinking about my attempts to impress Sarah on the jungle gym still makes me laugh."
3. **Ask About Experiences:** Engage with the child's experiences and feelings. "I remember being shy about talking to new people when I was your age. What's something you're enjoying right now?"
4. **Involve the Child:** Engage children in your activities to build shared understanding. "I'm making my schedule for today. Let's come up with a drawing or poem to put on the refrigerator together."

Social Skills Milestones

- **Birth - 6 months:** Responds to social interactions with smiles and coos.
- **6 - 12 months:** Develops attachment to caregivers, starts to show fear of strangers.
- **12 - 24 months:** Shows a range of emotions, begins to play simple games like peek-a-boo.
- **2 - 3 years:** Plays alongside other children (parallel play), begins to understand turn-taking.

Encouraging Social and Emotional Growth

Parents can encourage social and emotional development by:

- **Creating a Safe Environment:** Ensuring children feel safe to express their emotions.
- **Modeling Positive Behavior:** Demonstrating empathy and positive social interactions.
- **Engaging in Interactive Play:** Encouraging games and activities that require cooperation and sharing.

Conclusion

Understanding and supporting social and emotional development is crucial for building a child's confidence and empathy. Regular interactions, modeling positive behavior, and providing a secure environment help foster these essential skills.

CHAPTER 6

Factors Affecting Development

Child development is influenced by a myriad of factors, which together shape the course of a child's growth and learning. These factors include genetic endowment, environmental influences, health, and nutrition. Each plays a vital role in determining the types of connections formed in the brain and the overall developmental trajectory.

The Role of Genetics and Environment

Genetic Factors: Genetic endowment is akin to a baby's first curriculum, the blueprint they are born with. This genetic makeup includes traits like eye color, artistic ability, and a tendency towards certain aptitudes. While genetics provide the framework, they do not dictate a child's characteristics in isolation. Instead, they interact with the environment to mold individual growth and development.

Environmental Factors: The environment a child grows up in plays a crucial role in their development. A safe, stimulating environment encourages healthy growth, whereas overcrowded or understimulating settings can hinder progress. For example, children living in war zones or extreme poverty often face developmental challenges due to continuous feelings of unsafety.

Interactions Between Genetics and Environment: Genetics and environment together shape a child's development. For instance, while a child may be genetically predisposed to excel in a certain area, without the right environmental support, this potential may not be fully realized. Conversely, supportive environments can help mitigate genetic vulnerabilities.

Genetics and Environment

"Genetic endowment is the equivalent of a baby's first developmental course - the curriculum that came with the brain at birth. Genetics examine, throughout development, variability in abilities, and at each age, it offers a window into the strength and limitations of any given individual in any given domain of development" (Schofield-Tomschin et al., 2010, p. 44). Properties like eye/hair color, artistic ability, or a tendency toward math and science are attributed to biological processes. This natural course of growth is determined from birth.

Environmental Impact: Children can grow and learn optimally if their environments support their needs. While some children may have favorable conditions that allow them to thrive, others may face risks due to prenatal, perinatal, or postnatal environmental factors.

The Importance of Health and Nutrition

Health Factors: Regular health check-ups, accurate prescriptions, and testing for conditions like lead exposure are vital for maintaining a healthy developmental trajectory. Illnesses and diseases can significantly impact a child's learning and development.

Nutritional Factors: Nutrition is crucial for cognitive, psychological, social, and emotional development. Up to 20% of children in the United States show evidence of nutritional deficiencies, which can lead to developmental delays. Conversely, overnutrition can result in overstimulation and abnormal development patterns.

Nutrition and Health

In child development, nutrition is a significant factor. A poor diet can reduce overall health, leading to negative developmental outcomes. Good nutrition is harder to achieve in children who are frequently ill, which can create a cycle of poor health and compromised nutrition.

Impact of Malnutrition: Malnutrition is linked to developmental delay and decreased immunity, contributing to poor health outcomes. Studies show that children from poorer homes tend to be shorter, lighter, and have poorer motor coordination compared to their wealthier counterparts. Early nutrition quality significantly determines health, cognitive, and physical outcomes.

Research Findings: Research indicates that poor-quality nutrition can negatively impact a child's cognitive abilities, academic achievement, and future job prospects. For instance, the Goodger study (2005) in New Zealand found that birth weight, heavily influenced by prenatal and postnatal nutrition, was a significant predictor of a premature baby's IQ score.

Economic Implications: Improved nutrition can lead to significant economic benefits by reducing healthcare costs and enhancing productivity. A 2003 report estimated that better nutrition could reduce acute illness costs by $68 million to $154 million annually for children in Australia.

CHAPTER 7

Monitoring and Celebrating Milestones

L ife is full of moments, both big and small, that deserve to be documented. Every birthday, every "first," and every memorable event usually gets marked in some way—be it a photo, a handwritten note, or a mental log entry. One of the most significant events in life—bringing a child into the world—brings multiple memorable moments. These moments, known as developmental milestones, plot the child's journey from baby to fully-functional human being. This makes them not only worth noting but also worth celebrating in some way.

The Importance of Monitoring Milestones

One of the biggest reasons for monitoring milestones is to ensure that a child is on their critical developmental path. Generally, if a child is making the right progress at the right time, they are in good health. However, if a child doesn't meet certain milestones, it doesn't necessarily indicate major problems. Development timelines are flexible, and delays might be simple to address or just variations in normal brain development.

Celebrating Milestones

Marking and celebrating milestones can be a joyful experience. These celebrations can vary from simple acknowledgments to larger family gatherings, providing a sense of accomplishment for the child and creating lasting memories.

Ways to Celebrate Milestones

- **Documenting Firsts:** Capture photos, write notes, or keep a scrapbook to document significant firsts, such as the first step, first word, or first day of school.
- **Family Gatherings:** Organize a small celebration with family to mark important milestones. This could be as simple as a family dinner or a small party.
- **Trophies and Awards:** Consider giving a child a small trophy or award for achievements like the first successful potty training or learning to ride a bike.
- **Homemade Booklets:** Create a special page in a homemade booklet for each milestone. This can include drawings, photos, and written descriptions of the event.
- **Interactive Celebrations:** Engage the child in activities to celebrate their milestones, such as drawing a picture together or making a craft.

Encouragement and Support

Celebrating milestones not only marks the child's progress but also encourages further development. Positive reinforcement and support from family and caregivers play a crucial role in a child's growth and confidence.

Conclusion

Monitoring and celebrating developmental milestones provide a comprehensive view of a child's growth and create cherished memories. By recognizing and celebrating these achievements, parents and caregivers contribute to the child's overall development and well-being.

CHAPTER 8

Common Concerns and Red Flags

While presenting a general idea of what milestones to expect for a child's development during the first five years of life, it's important to address the concerns that parents or caregivers might have about their individual child's development. There may be a history of developmental delays in the family, or specific circumstances surrounding a child's birth or health that cause worry. For those who are anxious, it's critical to consult a professional about any concerns.

Understanding Developmental Variations

Children develop at different rates, and what is presented here represents average ages at which most children meet milestones. This guide includes skills mastered by 85-90% of children of a given age, but there is a wide range of "normal." This is why it's best to consult a professional when there are doubts.

Importance of Early Identification

Identifying developmental delays as early as possible can greatly benefit a child. Early intervention services exist to help children experiencing difficulties or delays in vision, hearing, speech, fine and gross motor abilities, social skills, cognition, or learning. Knowing the warning signs in all these areas is crucial.

Recognizing Developmental Delays

The challenge for some parents is when their baby or young child is not yet doing many of the basics mentioned. Traits such as ignoring social rules or saying "no" frequently are not true developmental delays; they may just be part of personality development.

Key Areas of Concern

- **Vision and Hearing:** Delays in these areas can be subtle. Parents should watch for lack of response to visual or auditory stimuli.
- **Speech and Language:** Delays might include limited vocabulary, difficulty forming sentences, or not responding to spoken language.
- **Motor Skills:** Difficulties in crawling, walking, or using hands effectively can indicate delays in fine and gross motor skills.
- **Social Skills:** Lack of interest in interacting with others or difficulty understanding social cues can be signs of delay.
- **Cognitive Skills:** Problems with memory, problem-solving, or learning new tasks might suggest cognitive delays.

Professional Consultation

If any concerns arise, it is crucial to consult with a pediatrician or a developmental specialist. They can provide screenings and assessments to determine if there are significant delays and recommend appropriate interventions.

Conclusion

While milestones provide a general framework, individual variations are expected. Early identification and intervention can make a significant difference in a child's development. It's always better to consult a professional when in doubt.

www.ingramcontent.com/pod-product-compliance
Lightning Source LLC
Chambersburg PA
CBHW021406160726
47994CB00007B/3095